Restore My Soul

Restore My Soul
A GRIEF COMPANION

LORRAINE
PETERSON

NAVPRESS
BRINGING TRUTH TO LIFE
P.O. Box 35001, Colorado Springs, Colorado 80935

OUR GUARANTEE TO YOU

We believe so strongly in the message of our books that we are making this quality guarantee to you. If for any reason you are disappointed with the content of this book, return the title page to us with your name and address and we will refund to you the list price of the book. To help us serve you better, please briefly describe why you were disappointed. Mail your refund request to: NavPress, P.O. Box 35002, Colorado Springs, CO 80935.

The Navigators is an international Christian organization. Our mission is to reach, disciple, and equip people to know Christ and to make Him known through successive generations. We envision multitudes of diverse people in the United States and every other nation who have a passionate love for Christ, live a lifestyle of sharing Christ's love, and multiply spiritual laborers among those without Christ.

NavPress is the publishing ministry of The Navigators. NavPress publications help believers learn biblical truth and apply what they learn to their lives and ministries. Our mission is to stimulate spiritual formation among our readers.

FOR A FREE CATALOG OF
NAVPRESS BOOKS & BIBLE STUDIES,
CALL 1-800-366-7788 (USA)
OR 1-416-499-4615 (CANADA)

CONTENTS

ACKNOWLEDGMENTS

With this book I remember my mother, Gladys Skog Peterson. Even when I was a child, she shared with me the feelings she experienced as an eighteen-year-old when her father was suddenly killed in a car accident. "People avoided me because they didn't know what to say," she'd recall. "But I only wanted to know that they cared." Her compassion for the grieving and her special talent for showing her concern in appropriate and practical ways left its mark on me.

When I was in high school, I started writing letters to bereaved people—something I continue to this day. I felt that those who don't enjoy writing as much as I do might appreciate a special message to give to a friend or a relative who has lost a loved one. What I've lived vicariously through the grieving people I've tried to comfort and experienced personally in my own losses has found its way into this book. The input of my talented and sensitive editor, David Hazard, whose own mother died recently from cancer, has substantially improved the manuscript.

But it's God who has made *Restore My Soul* possible. If it weren't for the hope of eternal life He offers, the love He expresses in so many ways, the comfort He gives, and the ability He has to restore broken hearts, there would be nothing to write about.

INTRODUCTION:
A COMPANION IN GRIEF

LOSING someone we love is perhaps the most painful, overwhelming experience of life. Many of us experience a stunning mixture of emotional and spiritual states—from sadness to anger, from faith to despair. These moods move through us like weather fronts, so we find ourselves one moment placid, a short time later buffeted by an interior storm. Moreover, we can feel so vulnerable to these rapid changes—or so tired of covering them in the presence of others—that we keep ourselves apart and alone. And so we compound our grief with emotional isolation.

To be alone in our sorrow is not necessarily bad. A certain amount of time on our own is needed. Time to let true feelings rise and be dealt with. Time to let life re-sort itself. But sometimes we need assistance with the reorganizing. Without help, emotions can become overwhelming; a new and different view of the future can be paralyzing.

This little book is meant to be a type of "grief companion." Of course it doesn't substitute for the company of close friends and relatives in the all-important evaluating process that grief requires of us. But friends and family are not always available at the moment we need them. Sometimes we must do our own reflecting. In any case, getting a handle on our emotions and redrawing the "map" of our life is, after all, work that we must do for ourselves.

With this in mind, I offer this book of devotional readings as a "personal companion"—a guide for facing and understanding feelings and for thinking through new ways to cope with your life in the aftermath of loss. In my own times of overwhelming grief, this kind of simple but necessary "soul work" helped me recover my balance and go on with living.

You may wish to keep a small notebook with you as you read and reflect on each of the thirty-one entries. You may find it very helpful to write down your thoughts and feelings. You may wish to keep some of these questions in mind as you read:

- Which feelings do I identify with?

- Does the Scripture given offer ways to handle these feelings? What are they?

- How can I face the emotions I have . . . without letting them completely overwhelm or control me?

- Which aspect of God's character can I focus on, in order to keep my feelings in perspective?

- What truth from God's Word can I meditate on when unwanted ideas fill my mind?

- Is there some action I should pursue, a new attitude I must take, to enable me to move through grief? What steps will I take today to help that change begin?

- What wisdom and insight have I gained—about life, myself, people, or God?

Some days you may not feel like writing anything. Some entries may not stir much of a response. Only you can strike the balance between "forcing" yourself to write when it would not be helpful and "disciplining" yourself by writing just a little, which often prompts the words to flow (like priming an old well pump) when you don't think you have anything to say. (Or when you just don't *want* to say anything!)

Apart from these more mechanical aspects of personal writing, I'm quite sure that recording your thoughts and feelings will help in several important ways. First, you'll find it very helpful—and healthy—to unburden your soul. Writing openly and honestly "gets your feelings out"—and "out" is a good place for heavy, painful inner energies to be. Second, over time you'll notice the shape of your thoughts changing and the sharp edges of painful feelings smoothing. There is comfort and encouragement in knowing that you're taking steps ahead.

Just as important, you will find yourself gaining wisdom and insight. It's possible you will deepen your understanding—of

God, of other people's struggles, of what's important to you in life . . . and perhaps you'll receive new light on your future.

And so I leave you—not on your own, but in hands far more skilled than mine—to walk the journey through grief . . . to a new life that may be hard to see right now, though it lies just ahead. . . .

IT CAN'T BE

IT's only a nightmare, isn't it? The one with whom I shared so much has passed away—never to talk, never to hug, never to laugh again. It can't be! The person who understood my heartaches, rejoiced at my good fortune, and helped me face tomorrow is gone forever. Of course I knew that death would strike close—sometime. But it's more than I can handle now. Lost in a world of tears, pain, and uncertainty, I'm not sure which way to turn.

And so I turn to You, O God. I need to know You are near me. I ask You to steady me . . . strengthen me . . . as I cry out to You and as I let Your Word speak to my soul:

> Save me, O God, . . . I sink in the miry depths,
> where there is no foothold. I have come into the
> deep waters; the floods engulf me. (Psalm 69:1-2)

Hear my cry, O God; listen to my prayer. From the ends of the earth I call to you, I call as my heart grows faint; lead me to the rock that is higher than I. For you have been my refuge, a strong tower. . . . I long to dwell in your tent forever and take refuge in the shelter of your wings. (Psalm 61:1-4)

Yet this I call to mind and therefore I have hope: Because of the LORD's great love [I am] not consumed, for his compassions never fail. (Lamentations 3:21-22)

The eternal God is [my] refuge, and underneath are the everlasting arms. (Deuteronomy 33:27)

PRAYER
LORD, be my Refuge and my Shelter. Reach down in compassion and be my Reason to hope again.

WHY?

I'M overwhelmed by sadness. My heart physically aches.

Some days my loss dominates each waking hour, interrupting my work and invading my fantasies. My routine is filled with reminders of unpleasant changes. I pass a favorite spot. Pick up an old card or letter and see that familiar writing. Recall our last words spoken together. Each memory is like a whisper saying, *Life will never be the same.*

In the face of bereavement, some say, "The Lord gives and the Lord takes away." Easy for them. Right now, I can only agonize, *Why? Why give . . . then take away?*

Now I am faced with a new need. A need to let God give me wisdom and understanding greater than my questions. I need Him to help me understand the wisdom that drives His action . . . that set this world and all life in motion . . . that knows when to give and when to take away.

And while I desire to be open to this new understanding, I need to know, O God, Your presence with me even more. And so I seek understanding—and Your comfort—in Your Word:

> My heart is not proud, O LORD, my eyes are not haughty; I do not concern myself with great matters or things too wonderful for me. But I have stilled and quieted my soul; like a weaned child with its mother, like a weaned child is my soul within me. (Psalm 131:1-2)

> Even though I walk through the valley of the shadow of death, I will fear no evil, for you are with me; your rod and your staff, they comfort me. (Psalm 23:4)

> Let the beloved of the LORD rest secure in him, for he shields him all day long, and the one the LORD loves rests between his shoulders. (Deuteronomy 33:12)

PRAYER

LORD, fill me with the peace that is beyond all human understanding. Help me surrender my *whys* as I trust in Your greater wisdom . . . and know Your comfort.

HOW CAN I FACE THE FUTURE?

WHEN I think about my loss, I feel such grief for the *dreams* that will never be realized. For the hope that evaporated in a moment. For *plans* that can never be accomplished. It's as if our shared experiences formed a beautiful object made of crystal, and now it's shattered. These memories are like the broken pieces, too painful to pick up. The life that could have been cannot be put back together again.

And so I am left to wonder, *How can I face my future?*

Where can I turn, heartbroken and confused . . . often not even caring about tomorrow? How can I find the will to go on?

God, I know that You are the Great Designer, the One who has all my *tomorrows* under control. Help me to trust You as the architect of what *will* be—the One capable of creating something beautiful out of that which is broken.

I will listen today, when You say to me:

> "For I know the plans I have for you," declares the
> LORD, "plans to prosper you and not to harm you,
> plans to give you hope and a future."
> (Jeremiah 29:11)

> "Like clay in the hand of the potter," [declares the
> LORD], "so are you in my hand." (Jeremiah 18:6)

> He heals the brokenhearted and binds up their
> wounds. (Psalm 147:3)

PRAYER

LORD, pick up the pieces of my life—my today and my
tomorrow—and reshape them into something new.
Help me overcome my fear of the future. Show me
how to trust You to lead me . . . step by step . . .
each new day.

MY INNER STRENGTH IS GONE

AT times exhaustion overtakes me. I may have the energy to do what's expected of me—even to rise to the occasion.

But then a fog of tiredness creeps in. My thoughts are weary and confused. My body aches from fatigue.

Then comes a sense of . . . *meaninglessness*—an inability to focus. And I wonder does my work—or any work—really matter any more?

Maybe there are others who face their loss and just "get on with life." I'm not one of them. My passion and zest for living have evaporated.

Where will my purpose and strength come from, God, if not from You? Where will my new reason to go on come from, if not from You? Made from the dust of the earth, I am dependent on the power of the Holy Spirit within me to give me the resources I so desperately need in order to cope.

Help me, today, to depend on and draw strength from You alone. Let today be an opportunity to grow closer to You—to find my reason for being in You only. I turn to Your Word, to find strength in my weakness:

> As a father has compassion on his children, so the LORD has compassion on those who fear him; for he knows how we are formed, he remembers that we are dust. (Psalm 103:13-14)

> In my distress I called to the LORD. . . . Salvation comes from [him]. (Jonah 2:2,9)

> Surely God is my salvation; I will trust and not be afraid. . . . With joy [I] will draw water from the wells of salvation. (Isaiah 12:2-3)

PRAYER

LORD, remember that I am made of dust. Show me Your compassion and Your love. Help me to find new strength in new purpose.

5

I FEEL SUCH EMPTINESS

SOME days have passed and, as the numbness subsides, I notice that a part of me has died, too.

Sometimes I feel so completely empty. It makes me anxious, even panicky. I rush around, trying to distract myself with noise and busyness.

All I seem able to do is to return to my memories—of that smile, that touch, those talents and abilities that added so much to my life. I replay conversations. Relive moments when that special caring made me feel . . . full. Then the memory goes. Only a gapping void remains. The air, empty. Something I will never be able to replace is gone.

Today I think, *How carefully and how wonderfully each one of us is made.* No one can ever fill the place left by another. How fortunate I was to have enjoyed this unique person—even if I wish the time could have been extended.

How priceless was the gift of this life to me.

Today, too, I will let go of this beloved gift that was given by God, and returned to God. Some day we'll be reunited—never to part again. For the present, I will hope in God. I'll find my fullness in His Word:

> He has also set eternity in the hearts of men . . .
> the dust returns to the ground it came from, and
> the spirit returns to God who gave it.
> (Ecclesiastes 3:11; 12:7)

> So God created man in his own image, . . . male and
> female he created them. (Genesis 1:27)

> Therefore we are always confident and know that
> as long as we are at home in the body we are away
> from the Lord. We live by faith, not by sight. We
> are confident, I say, and would prefer to be away
> from the body and at home with the Lord.
> (2 Corinthians 5:6-8)

PRAYER

LORD, help me not to dwell on old memories and live in past realities. Help me to find my life in the present, in the living . . . and in You. Give me Your eternal perspective on my future.

6

I'M SO FRAGILE

I see myself as a generally solid person. And yet . . .

I don't seem to have much resilience right now. I can be strong one moment, but then something inside drops like a rag doll that's lost its stuffing. I'm vulnerable to sentimental things. I can't deal with stress or pressure. I feel like I could snap at the slightest provocation.

Every challenge seems too big. Molehills are mountains. Cracks in the sidewalk of life might as well be chasms. I feel so foolish, and yet unable to do anything about this inner fragility.

Is it possible for You, Lord, to take away the "shattered" feeling? Is it possible for You to be the companionship, love, security, and sense of belonging that made me feel strong and whole before? I'm glad the answer is "yes," because I need an emotional reserve from beyond myself.

How good to know I can draw strength from You and Your Word, O God:

> "A bruised reed he will not break, and a smoldering wick he will not snuff out." (Isaiah 42:3)

> I pray that you, being rooted and established in [God's] love, may have power, together with all the saints, to grasp how wide and long and high and deep is the love of Christ, and to know this love that surpasses knowledge—that you may be filled to the measure of all the fullness of God. (Ephesians 3:17-19)

> For in Christ all the fullness of the Deity lives in bodily form, and you have been given fullness in Christ. (Colossians 2:9-10)

PRAYER

LORD, help me to realize that You love me completely . . . and that as I trust in You I will find a new kind of inner strength I've never known before.

7

IF ONLY...

IF only I had a second chance.

I keep thinking of what I should have said—words of encouragement, appreciation, forgiveness, or gratitude. My mind is filled with things I could have done—taken time to listen, gone out of my way a bit, overlooked a fault, or helped when it was needed. At times the thought torments me— *Too late.*

It's tempting to try to justify my negligence. *I was too busy. I "meant" to. I would have someday.* But it doesn't help. I can't find a "good enough" reason, and I get down on myself. *What was wrong with me? Why didn't I?*

Today I need to know there is wisdom in moving on and finding my "second chances" in new places and new circumstances, with other people. And there is comfort in knowing that God, whose compassion for us never fails, offers us new opportunities everywhere. I can pray, *Lord, forgive me for the past. Let me have only enough regret for the things I left undone yesterday . . . to teach me how to show kindness, thoughtfulness, generosity, and support to someone today.*

Yes, I need to feel safe in God's forgiving presence and to know I have His understanding and pardon. That way I'm free from the prison of the past, and I can move on, looking for chances to help, to encourage, and to care. I can live with a new priority—to reflect God's love, joy, peace, patience, and goodness . . . to make each day better for someone else.

Even through tough reminders, I can be thankful that God can use *everything* in this life for good. The truths I will live by come from the Bible:

> "Forget the former things; do not dwell on the past," [says the LORD]. "See, I am doing a new thing! Now it springs up; do you not perceive it? I am making a way in the desert and streams in the wasteland." (Isaiah 43:18-19)

> Therefore, as we have opportunity, let us do good to all people, especially to those who belong to the family of believers. (Galatians 6:10)

PRAYER

LORD, I cannot continue to relive the past. Help me to make the most of every moment, every opportunity. Open my eyes and give me the chance to reflect Your goodness to someone today.

MEMORIES ARE NO LONGER MY FRIENDS

ALMOST at every turn, I meet a new enemy. A joke we both laughed at. A TV program we enjoyed together. The perfect greeting card that wouldn't fit anyone else. A reminder of a special day we spent together.

These memories have lost their beauty. They aren't comforting; they're painful. Sometimes they bring tears to my eyes.

Who can I turn to but You, God? I don't want to hear advice like, "Just be glad for the time you had together." It doesn't help. I trust You know that. But . . . can You begin to mend my heart? I need to begin the slow process of healing inside, so that my treasure stock of memories will gradually stop being a source of distress. I want to stop avoiding them—and to know I can carry them with me into the future.

Today I need to be confident that the God who created the best times of my past is planning good times ahead. I need to thank Him for the gift of memory—and of *good* memories. I look to God's promises to find the way to ensure great moments that I will always want to remember:

> The Lord himself goes before you and will be with you; he will never leave you nor forsake you. Do not be afraid; do not be discouraged.
> (Deuteronomy 31:8)

> "And surely, I am with you always."
> (Matthew 28:20)

PRAYER

LORD, help me to face the memories that cause me grief. I trust You to once again make my memories from the past a source of joy . . . and in the days ahead to create wonderful new memories for the future.

9

I'M LOST

The best way to describe myself right now is . . . like a lost child.

It's like some great storm blew in and swept away all that was familiar, cherished, dependable. Like the world turned upside down.

There are moments—whole days—when I go from numb to fearful, to exhausted. I'm tempted to resign from life. But there is no giving up, no place to stop or hide. So I go on, driven by the day's schedule, the calendar, and necessity.

The question is *Where am I going?* It seems as if I'm wandering into the uncharted unknown to face forces I can't see.

Not only does this sense of being lost cause me turmoil and panic, it also makes me feel ridiculous. I'm a grown human being. I never thought I would lose my way.

In the midst of this lostness, I need to know there is someone I can rely on to seek me and find me—to walk with me—

even when I'm not sure where I'm going. That Someone is You, God. I pause now and listen to Your Word:

> "Do not fear, for I am with you; do not be dismayed, for I am your God. I will strengthen you and help you; I will uphold you with my . . . right hand." (Isaiah 41:10)

> "Peace I leave with you; my peace I give you. I do not give to you as the world gives. Do not let your hearts be troubled and do not be afraid." (John 14:27)

> God has said, "Never will I leave you; never will I forsake you." (Hebrews 13:5)

PRAYER

LORD, You are the only one who knows where I am and where I'm headed. Let me begin to sense Your guiding hand upon me. I choose the path of faith instead of fear, trusting you to lead me toward new . . . and pleasant places.

MY SOUL IS
IN TURMOIL

SOME days I wake feeling strong and at peace . . . but by the end of the day I'm in turmoil.

I begin to see what undermines me: I compare my circumstances to those who haven't lost. I think of what might have been. I look at the changes ahead—the future that will not turn out as I planned it. Sadness and bitterness set in. Or fear and worry.

And then there are the nights I lie awake, tossing and turning until dawn. I look at the past and think, *If only. . . .* I look ahead to the future and feel a cold sweat, thinking, *What if . . . ?*

No one but God can calm the turmoil in my soul. Only God can help me to stop borrowing upset and trouble by looking at others in different circumstances. Only He can help me to accept my situation, because in truth, it cannot be changed.

Likewise, only God can help me to see the pointlessness of looking back at "things as they might have been" and of looking ahead to imagined terrors that "might be."

And so I give God everything: my anxious thoughts, my concerns . . . my whole life. He alone holds the past in His hand, as well as the future. If God knows the end from the beginning, if *this* wonderful God is my Father, then what do I have to fear? The One whose eternal plan was to send His Son, Jesus Christ, to redeem me—how can His plan for my future bring anything but peace and goodness?

God invites me to live calmly . . . in quiet tranquility and contentment . . . *in the present*. And so I'll settle my soul on eternal truth from the Scriptures, which tell me:

> You will keep in perfect peace him whose mind is steadfast, because he trusts in you. (Isaiah 26:3)

> Let the peace of Christ rule in your hearts, since as members of one body you were called to peace. And be thankful. (Colossians 3:15)

> Do not be anxious about anything, but in everything, by prayer and petition, with thanksgiving, present your requests to God. And the peace of God, which transcends all understanding, will guard your hearts and your minds in Christ Jesus. (Philippians 4:6-7)

PRAYER

LORD, I am Yours. Take care of me from this day on. I want You to be my God, and to let Your peace guard my heart. Today, and every day, I will let go and allow You to be God. I will seek Your help and guidance, trusting You to lead me . . . in peace.

//

I DON'T WANT
TO BE BITTER

HAVE you ever wanted the chance to face God and get Him to answer some questions? I have. In times when my soul is bleak with grief I want to ask: God, if You're all-powerful, why do You allow suffering and death? Why allow tragedy and heartbreak? Why is it that some people are given to live in relative peace, health, and ease, while others of us are handed sickness and bitter loss?

Are You sure You knew what You were doing when You took the one I loved away from me?

I recognize that leaving spiritual questions hidden in my soul—and unasked—is an open invitation to bitterness. And *that* I don't want. But to even begin addressing them I need wisdom from far beyond me.

So I turn to those with more knowledge and spiritual insight. I consider Job, who complained bitterly . . . and whose dark questions vanished in the light of Your great appearing. I reflect on the psalmist, who angrily doubted Your justice . . . and who concluded: "Whom have I in heaven but you? And earth has nothing I desire besides you" (Psalm 73:25).

I go on to ponder the apostle Paul, who came to the end of human understanding, and declared: "Oh, the depth of the riches of the wisdom and knowledge of God! How unsearchable his judgments, and his paths beyond tracing out!" (Romans 11:33).

I've heard it said, "Sorrow can make you *bitter* or *better.*" I realize that I can remain frustrated and angry in the shadowy labyrinth of my thinking and my judgments as to the way life should be. Or I can place my trust in You and in the wisdom I find in Your Word—a wisdom that is eternal:

> But as for me, it is good to be near God. I have
> made the Sovereign LORD my refuge.
> (Psalm 73:28)

> "My thoughts are not your thoughts, neither are
> your ways my ways," declares the LORD. "As the
> heavens are higher than the earth, so are my ways
> higher than your ways and my thoughts than your
> thoughts." (Isaiah 55:8-9)

PRAYER

GOD—Sovereign Lord—I, too, take You as my refuge.
Because You can view things in the light of eternity
and I cannot, I choose to let You run the universe.
This includes my little world.

12

BE MY COMFORT

PEOPLE "mean well" . . . but they don't really understand. Sometimes they try to drag me to "fun things." They try to force jokes and laughter in an attempt to shake me out of my sadness.

At other times, their feeble, struggling attempts to console seem so awkward. They come with embarrassed expressions and stiff "I just want to express my sympathy" words. They offer cold comforts like, "You'll be better in a few weeks . . ." or ". . . you can't live in the past, you must go on."

Some have said, "If there's anything I can do, just let me know," but could I really call at 2:00 A.M. when I'm desperately lonely and need to talk to someone? Could I really ask them to accompany me when I go to the airport, the restaurant, or the mall . . . just so I don't have to go alone?

I know that others can't really walk in my shoes exactly. I know I can't expect them to offer what they're unable to give. And so I turn to the Lord, and hear Him say, "Be still, and know that I am God" (Psalm 46:10). Times like these teach me what the philosopher meant when he said that each of us has a God-shaped vacuum within, which only He can fill. These times teach me to turn to the Lord, to trust in Him, and to learn more about Him and His ways as I read the Word, which says:

> Praise be to the God and Father of our Lord Jesus Christ, the Father of compassion and the God of all comfort, who comforts us in all our troubles, so that we can comfort those in any trouble with the comfort we ourselves have received from God. (2 Corinthians 1:3-4)

> For everything that was written in the past was written to teach us, so that through endurance and the encouragement of the Scriptures we might have hope. (Romans 15:4)

PRAYER

LORD, be to me the "Father of compassion" and "the God of all comfort." Give me the gifts of tranquility and endurance as I seek come to know You in Your Word . . . and in my life.

MY FAITH IS WEAK

"IT was God's will."

"It was in God's perfect timing."

"Accept it."

People have no idea how light and empty those words can sound, even to another person of faith. *They* aren't the ones lying awake at night with an aching heart. They don't encounter the sharp reminders of emptiness each time they turn around. They didn't bury their dreams for the future.

I feel hurt and angry that someone I loved so much has been taken from me. I want some answers. I want to ask God some honest questions like: "How can You ask me to *trust* You when You didn't use Your power to prevent my distress?"

And yet, even as I ask that question, I know I have three choices to make. *First,* I have to decide who I'm willing to place my trust in: *God* or *myself. Second,* I have to decide if I'm fit to be God's judge . . . or if I am going to learn how to rest in the arms of a God who created all things. *Third,* I have to choose between believing that God's sovereign will is ultimately good even though it's far beyond my understanding . . . or I have to create a new belief that suits me.

When I stop and consider even the first choice, I'm not sure I should totally trust someone who loses the car keys, forgets appointments, and fails to keep promises. I'd never ask other people to place complete and utter confidence in me. Why would I put that much trust in myself, *especially* during this time when everything is shaken inside me . . . when I feel weak and battered and floundering?

So God, I will decide to put my trust in You. And the truth I choose to live by is found in Your Word:

> Without faith it is impossible to please God, because anyone who comes to him must believe that he exists and that he rewards those who earnestly seek him. (Hebrews 11:6)

> I do believe; help me overcome my unbelief! (Mark 9:24)

> Faith comes from hearing the message, and the message is heard through the word of Christ. (Romans 10:17)

PRAYER

LORD, I will place my trust in You alone. No matter the paths on which You choose to lead me, I trust You to be unchanging, reliable, full of love and justice. I believe that You will reward me if I earnestly seek You—even if I come bearing questions and doubts.

14

I'M SO DESPERATELY LONELY

ISOLATION . . . emptiness. . . . These are my only constant companions.

When I shop at a crowded mall or grocery store . . . loneliness hounds me. When I go to church I sit surrounded by people . . . but alone. A sense of detachment rudely interrupts my conversation with a friend.

No busyness, no distraction, not even the company of people I enjoy can free me from alienation for very long. It's as if there is an unseen barrier between me and other people. No one seems able to cross it, so no one can really understand my loss or empathize with my struggles.

But when I am utterly alone and desolate, the words of the psalmist echo in my mind: "My soul finds rest in God alone" (Psalm 62:1). And that makes me wonder, God, *do You allow such loneliness for a reason? Is it to drive us to You?* And this image comes to mind: "Even the sparrow has found a home . . . a place near your altar. . . . Blessed are those who dwell in your house" (Psalm 84:3-4).

And now I think that when the nest made of my human securities is destroyed, God calls me to Himself. And if I want to find my way to Him, I must let His Word guide me:

> Find rest, O my soul, in God alone; my hope comes from him. He alone is my rock and my salvation; he is my fortress, I will not be shaken. My salvation and my honor depend on God; he is my mighty rock, my refuge. Trust in him at all times, O people; pour out your hearts to him, for God is our refuge. (Psalm 62:5-8)

> Because your love is better than life, my lips will glorify you. I will praise you as long as I live, and in your name I will lift up my hands. My soul will be satisfied as with the richest of foods; with singing lips my mouth will praise you. (Psalm 63:3-5)

PRAYER

LORD, I will find my rest in You. I ask You to dispel my loneliness. Show me, today, how You alone can satisfy my soul.

15

HELP ME
FACE REALITY

SOMETIMES my mind plays tricks on me.

I forget that the one I loved and lost is no longer here. I find myself planning to tell some good news, to ask for advice, or to share a moment together. I imagine my loved one here with me.

Then comes the stony realization of how final death really is. How long will I continue to get these cold slaps?

I know that habits formed over years aren't easily broken. I know that the things I long for once more will shape my dreams and fantasies. The one I loved seems so alive and so close. Sometimes it's as if my dear departed one is standing at my side. But no . . .

I know that memory is one thing. But living mesmerized by dreams and wishes I project onto present reality is quite another. I almost expect the door to open and to see my loved one walking toward me. In my imagination I hear the voice that meant so much to me. Others have experienced similar feelings, so I know I'm not the only one . . . and I'm not "crazy."

Maybe there's something in me that just refuses to let go. I don't understand it . . . but I know God does. I know I can be sure of His stability and His compassion as I sort out the confusion of past and present in my head. I want to live in current reality. And so I turn to the Bible for comfort and help:

> O LORD, you have searched me and you know me. You know when I sit and when I rise; you perceive my thoughts from afar. . . . You are familiar with all my ways. . . . Where can I go from your Spirit? . . . If I rise on the wings of the dawn, if I settle on the far side of the sea, even there your hand will guide me, your right hand will hold me fast.
> (Psalm 139:1-3,7,9-10)

PRAYER

LORD, I open myself to You—sharing even these intrusions of unreality, which are so personal . . . and a little embarrassing. Help me to live in the present. I need You to direct my thoughts, so I am living current with *today.*

16

I DREAD THE "SPECIAL" DAYS

How will I get through the holidays . . . anniversaries . . . birthdays?

I used to anticipate these events with such happiness. Now I fight back tears whenever I merely think about special days that formed our family traditions. Now there's one less place to set at the table on holidays . . . fewer presents to buy . . . no one to make that special contribution to the occasion.

Am I supposed to celebrate when my heart is empty? Do I fake it? Or do I just sit alone, and let everyone else have a good time without having me around?

I do know that hibernation isn't for humans, but I just dread the thought of being surrounded by fun and happiness . . . and I don't know how to get through it.

And so I turn to God. I'm going to need His help. If I depend solely on my own willpower, I'll just put on a brave front . . . and never heal inside. I never really liked covering up anyway.

As I learn not to allow the past to affect the present, I will seek God for His help, so that the pain of my loss will not destroy the bright moments that are coming my way . . . forming a new future.

Taking life one day at the time, I want to learn how to rely on God's promises:

> "Moses, my servant, is dead. Now then, you and all these people, get ready to cross the Jordan River into the land I am about to give to them. . . . Have I not commanded you? Be strong and courageous. Do not be terrified; do not be discouraged, for the LORD your God will be with you wherever you go." (Joshua 1:2,9)

PRAYER

LORD, give me Your strength. Help me know how to face _____, a day I'd rather avoid. Help my soul rest in You. Help me fix my thoughts on the fact that You are the God who unfolds new days ahead of me . . . every one of them in Your plan. Give me the grace to experience peace . . . and joy.

FREE ME FROM SELF-PITY

I'VE been so preoccupied contemplating my loss . . . coping with my feelings . . . adjusting to my changed circumstances . . . getting used to my new responsibilities.

I haven't recognized how *self-absorbed* I've been. Some of it has been necessary. Some of it hasn't. It's true that I've had a new reality to sort out and overwhelming emotions to contend with—questions about everything from faith to friendships. But I'm tired of self-pity.

I don't think I have the resources—or the will—to center much attention on anyone but me. Yet I'm fed up with the days and nights I spend lost in my own head. I'm weary of being so enslaved to my own sadness that I feel uncomfortable in or avoid happy social settings. I'm tired of retreating into various levels of despair and depression every time I'm alone.

I know I must have divine intervention. I need God's help

to turn my face from the shadow toward the light again. I need an infusion of hope to deliver me from this sealed-off little world of myself and my problems.

Today I determine to begin following a path out to a whole world that lies beyond myself. I want to learn how to connect with, and care for, and receive love from other people again. To find my steps, I turn to the Book that has comforted and directed people throughout the ages:

> I heard and my heart pounded, my lips quivered at the sound; decay crept into my bones, and my legs trembled. Yet I will wait patiently for the day of calamity to come on the nation invading us. . . . I will rejoice in the LORD, I will be joyful in God my Savior. The Sovereign LORD is my strength; he makes my feet like the feet of a deer, he enables me to go on the heights. (Habakkuk 3:16,18-19)

PRAYER
LORD, help me to find true joy again in serving You . . . and others. Lead me out of this valley of shadow. Take me on to new heights of living.

18

I CAN'T HANDLE THESE RESPONSIBILITIES

THE loss was difficult enough to deal with. I wasn't expecting this sudden change in "job description," too.

It seems like every day I'm forced to face a new responsibility. A new decision that requires knowledge or experience I don't have. A new task I've never attempted before.

People offer help, but something in me hates constantly having to call on someone else. And the fact is, I'll have to learn to do these things by myself in time. Then I set out to tackle a job on my own . . . and I begin wishing the one I lost were here with me. Before I'm through, I've settled into a bad case of the blues again.

I hate this. It's not that I'm lazy or unwilling. But I used to feel competent and secure. Now I don't know what to do next. Along with that, I'm painfully aware that I could make some costly mistakes . . . but the relentless daily pressure of added responsibilities forces me on. And this *stop-the-world-I-want-to-get-off* attitude doesn't help.

To go on—to shoulder my new responsibilities well—I turn to God to sustain me. I need Him to make me strong and steady as I learn to handle roles I never thought I'd have to play. I take these Scripture passages literally, and apply them to my situation:

> I can do everything through him who gives me strength. (Philippians 4:13)

> Now to him who is able to do immeasurably more than all we ask or imagine, according to his power that is at work within us, to him be glory. (Ephesians 3:20-21)

> Not that we are competent in ourselves . . . but our competence comes from God. (2 Corinthians 3:5)

PRAYER

LORD, help me manage increased responsibility. Teach me to work quietly, in peace, and to depend totally on You for wisdom and strength. Show me the map for each day's travel, and help me to patiently do what I must do.

19

WILL LIFE EVER BE NORMAL AGAIN?

"TIME is a wonderful healer . . . and a terrible beautician."

I laughed the first time I heard this. Now it's not funny and I doubt that it is true. Time goes by. And I still feel pain and regret. I wish for the past . . . if only the one I've lost were here with me in the present. I long for what cannot be. I continue to feel uncomfortable around those who are experiencing life as usual.

Will I ever feel normal again?

I've tried to do things I enjoyed before. But when I do, they don't feel right. Within me there's this awkwardness, this twinge of guilt that ruins it all. If I launch into new areas of interest or attempt to meet new people, it feels like I'm trying too hard. And so I go between wanting to move on and feeling like I'm not ready to do so.

A concept from Scripture comes to mind: The Lord's ability ". . . to bind up the brokenhearted" (Isaiah 61:1). And so I am reminded: Only God can heal my emotions and restore my spirit . . . my joy for living.

Today I ask God to take charge of my social life and to work the inner changes necessary to make me feel wholly engaged with living again. I am thankful that He knows the simple steps I need to take, and that He allows me all the time I need. I put no stock in "time's" abilities to heal . . . and place my trust in the Lord's unlimited power. For in God's Word I read:

> The Spirit of the Sovereign LORD is on me, . . . He has sent me to bind up the brokenhearted, . . . to comfort all who mourn; . . . to bestow on them a crown of beauty instead of ashes, the oil of gladness instead of mourning, and a garment of praise instead of a spirit of despair. (Isaiah 61:1-3; see also Luke 4:18)

> You turned my wailing into dancing . . . and clothed me with joy. (Psalm 30:11)

PRAYER

LORD, help me to keep pace with *Your* healing process. Help me to be patient when it's slower than I would like. I give You permission to work any way You choose, as You renew my spirit . . . and set my life back on track.

20

I DON'T LIKE TO BE DEPENDENT

I don't mind trusting God—when things are going smoothly. But then I have everything under control. Why do I need faith?

Somehow self-reliance was drilled into me. I enjoy having people around but I hate to bother anyone or to ask for help. I'd rather do things on my own.

When I talk about trusting God, the truth is, I prefer to treat Him like a guy at the other end of the line when I need to make divine 911 calls. Good to have there, great to fall back on . . . in a total-panic kind of emergency.

But if I'm totally honest, I really dislike the idea of depending on a God I can't see or touch. I don't really like to be dependent on other people either—but then at least I have human arms around me . . . company with skin on it. I don't have the patience to pray and wait for "God's thoughts" on what to do about a faulty transmission, the important trip I'm planning, or the difficulty with a coworker. Somehow I feel that God's comfort, companionship, and advice just aren't enough.

Though it goes against all human reason, I know that I am strongest when I depend on God. I know that my aversion to depending on Him comes from my latent desire to have everything that spells security at my disposal so I rarely need to interrupt Him. But I ask, "Can a crisis improve my relationship with God?"—and answer in the affirmative.

As I learn a new, healthy dependence on God, I need to discover how to experience a deep sense of His love . . . and how to calmly await His solutions to my problems. So I turn to His Word and consider these truths:

> As for God, his way is perfect; the word of the LORD is flawless. He is a shield for all who take refuge in him. For who is God besides the LORD? And who is the Rock except our God? It is God who arms me with strength and makes my way perfect. . . . You give me your shield of victory, and your right hand sustains me; you stoop down to make me great. You broaden the path beneath me, so that my ankles do not turn.
> (Psalm 18:30-32,35-36)

PRAYER

LORD, I need assurance that You're really there—guiding me, sustaining me, and loving me. Broaden the path beneath my feet; make it solid . . . and teach me how to depend only on You.

21

HOW CAN LIFE JUST . . . GO ON?

I feel like I'm standing on a busy street, watching a parade go by. The theme of this parade is *Life Goes On.*

I'm not enjoying this. I can't get into it. I watch other people for whom it's "business as usual." I feel the need to push on, pressed by the tyranny of the urgent. But somehow I'm not *in* this life anymore. I'm like an observer. Disengaged.

When I look at the world, minus the one I loved, I feel sad. It's as if the sand has already blown over the mark made by this very special person. As every new day dawns, the memory of the person I miss so much fades in other people's minds. The roles filled—and the things done—are quickly being taken over by others as if nothing has happened. No, I don't expect the world to stop spinning. No, I'm not planning to build a "shrine" to force others to remember—but are we just cogs in a machine, so easily replaced? Doesn't a life have more significance than this? Am I the only one who senses a void that no one else can fill?

As I consider my own disengaged feeling, I come to think that maybe I'm using the wrong measuring stick to gauge the worth of the one I've lost. As long as I look to others, expecting them to assess the importance of that wonderful life, I am undoubtedly going to be disappointed.

Perhaps each of us can only leave a lasting effect on others as we live by values that are eternal—that is, by showing compassion, demonstrating integrity, sharing God's love in our words and actions. Could it be that our lasting memorials—sacrificial gifts that no one else sees, willingness to help a crabby neighbor, a refusal to take part in a dishonest business deal, simple faithfulness to family and friends—are only correctly evaluated by the eyes of God? Sure, because I was close to the one who's gone I could see and remember the great legacy left behind. So there is God, and me. Is it really so urgent that the world stop and take notice, too?

Today I see that God must wean me from needing other people's praises and approvals. Instead, I will let the eternal values that Jesus talked about be my standard:

> "But store up for yourselves treasures in heaven, where moth and rust do not destroy, and where thieves do not break in and steal." (Matthew 6:20)

PRAYER

LORD, thank You for the lasting memorials left by my loved one. Help me to live my life in a way that blesses others . . . and stores up treasures in heaven.

22

I NEED A GLIMPSE OF HEAVEN

I realize that when I "pity party" or when sad tears come to my eyes, I'm being somewhat selfish. When I think about it, I know the one lost to me is better off with You.

Maybe my reluctance to let God have possession of what has never been "mine" shows my self-centeredness. Surely He understands my weakness . . . my need to mourn.

As I return again and again to my feeling of loss, I also turn to the words Jesus spoke to the apostle Paul: "My grace is sufficient for you, for my power is made perfect in weakness" (2 Corinthians 12:9). I need that grace now . . . to help me rise *above* the here and now and let me catch a glimpse of heaven.

Today it eases my loss when I realize the pain of parting is only temporary. Sorrow is only for a season. This sad longing will end in happy reunion. How comforting to know that the one I love is at this moment enjoying God's presence, experiencing the beauty and peace of heaven, living in a place unmarred by sickness, sorrow, and death. How thankful I am that this is a destiny I'll be able to share.

This is the "vision" I long to hold on to—this glimpse beyond time, into eternity. I *need* the hope of heaven. And I'm thankful for these peace-bringing words:

> They will be his people, and God himself will be
> with them and be their God. He will wipe every tear
> from their eyes. There will be no more death or
> mourning or crying or pain, for the old order of
> things has passed away. (Revelation 21:3-4)

> "Do not let your hearts be troubled. . . . In my
> Father's house are many rooms; . . . I am going
> there to prepare a place for you . . . I will come back
> and take you to be with me that you also may be
> where I am." (John 14:1-3)

PRAYER

LORD, enable me to see beyond this day . . . this life. Help me to live in the light of heaven's reality. Thank You that, though the one I love can't return to me, someday we will be together again.

I WANT TO
BE THANKFUL

TODAY as I think about my loss, that word keeps circling in the back of my head: *Unfair!*

I've heard it said, "If all else fails, consider all that you have to be thankful for." I've never been very good at "counting my blessings."

On the other hand, today is a good day to start—so:

I am thankful for material things that make my life easier.

I am thankful for the friends and relatives who have supported me.

I am grateful for what the one who is gone meant to my life: words, humor, advice, example, kindness—and love—will always be mine to treasure. Most of all, I'm thankful that this life is not all there is . . . and that God has not abandoned me to live completely alone. I would like to express my gratitude for hope of a happy reunion with all the dear departed ones who knew Jesus Christ as Savior and Lord. This assurance penetrates my questioning and restlessness . . . bringing peace.

Sometimes it's still true that memories bring tears. But if I turn to God with thankfulness, then empty sorrow can turn to gratitude. I love the way His Word guides me from sadness to a thankful heart:

> "He who sacrifices thank offerings honors me, and he prepares the way so that I may show him the salvation of God." (Psalm 50:23)

> Give thanks in all circumstances, for this is God's will for you in Christ Jesus. (1 Thessalonians 5:18)

PRAYER

LORD, I don't always feel like giving thanks . . . but I sacrifice my easily given-into preoccupation with sorrow in order to give You well-deserved thanks. Thank You for future hope . . . for pleasant memories of the past . . . for Your presence here and now.

24

FORGIVE ME . . . AND HELP ME FORGIVE

I wasn't expecting death to unleash such strong reactions from so deep inside. Today I encounter memories better forgotten. Attitudes I've never dealt with. Buried pain. Guilt.

There are some important issues left unresolved. I find myself blaming my lost loved one for hurting me in certain ways. I condemn myself for the hurt and selfishness I dealt out. And I find the blaming attitude spreading as I think of others who let me down or made my life difficult.

I never thought forgiving would be part of grieving. But I see that I will need God's help so I can offer pardon, because blame is weighing me down. I turn to Him now, to receive strength and the power to forgive:

> See to it that no one misses the grace of God, and that no bitter root grows up to cause trouble and defile many. (Hebrews 12:15)

"Forgive us our debts as we also have forgiven our debtors." (Matthew 6:12)

"I am the vine; you are the branches. . . . Apart from me you can do nothing." (John 15:5)

Be kind and compassionate to one another, forgiving each other, just as in Christ God forgave you. (Ephesians 4:32)

PRAYER

LORD, for actions and attitudes contrary to Your will, I ask Your pardon. Give me Your ability to forgive. Help me forgive others—and myself—for being imperfect. Let me begin to reflect Your peace, patience, love . . . and pardon.

25

HOW CAN THEY
FORGET SO QUICKLY?

THE news stunned them into silence and sadness. At the funeral there were tears. They spoke so compassionately. They said all the right things and offered their help.

Now the calendar page has flipped to a new day . . . and that's *that*. Their lives are filled with busyness and laughter. It's as if they never made promises. I feel like a sad, unnoticed spectator unable to join the conversation, to participate in the planning, or to put my heart into my work. I'm so tempted to believe that their words were empty nothings. And that's painful. How can they forget so quickly?

And yet, God seems to remind me that I cannot sit in the judgment seat on this issue. (Or any issue, for that matter.) In the past, haven't I been just like everyone else—too busy, or just unable, to empathize with the widowed, the childless, the fatherless? Now the Lord seems to be teaching me not to expect from others what only He can impart, but to look only to Him for total understanding, true compassion, and unconditional love.

God seems to be reminding me that human words—though comforting—will never have the same power as His Word when it comes to renewing the spirit. And so I consider:

> It is better to take refuge in the LORD than to trust in man. (Psalm 118:8)

> "Blessed is the man who trusts in the LORD, whose confidence is in him. He will be like a tree planted by the water that sends out its roots by the stream. It does not fear when heat comes; its leaves are always green. It has no worries in a year of drought and never fails to bear fruit." (Jeremiah 17:7-8)

PRAYER

LORD, keep me from looking to people so intently for the understanding and security that only You can give. I want to be a tree with roots that constantly draw strength and life . . . from Your river of love and eternal truth.

26

HELP ME TO
LEARN FROM LOSS

SOMEONE has said, "Don't waste your sorrow"—which means, *from every loss learn how to live better.*

Sounds like good advice. And so I wonder, *What does death have to teach about life?*

First, I've found myself face to face with ultimate realities, and things formerly important have faded into insignificance. Second, I've been made to reevaluate my priorities. And as I follow through on the things I now see as important I will, in time, become a stronger and more focused person. My great loss is a constant reminder of my own mortality—silent evidence that one great purpose of this life is to prepare for the one to come.

How will I keep from "wasting" this sorrow?

I'll live each day remembering that, when I breathe my last, my genuine service to God and to others is the blessing that will remain. As I consider this fact, my preoccupation with "busyness" and pursuit of an easy life fall into perspective.

What I really want is God's help in choosing the path of my life from this day on. I want to live to do His will, to plan each day with eternity's values in view. I want God's words to direct my life:

> For to me, to live is Christ and to die is gain.
> (Philippians 1:21)

> Command them to do good, to be rich in good deeds, and to be generous and willing to share. In this way they will lay up treasure for themselves as a firm foundation for the coming age, so that they may take hold of the life that is truly life.
> (1 Timothy 6:18-19)

> Set your hearts on things above, where Christ is seated at the right hand of God. (Colossians 3:1)

PRAYER

LORD, help me to order my priorities so that they conform to Your plan for my life. Rather than investing my energy—and my substance—in getting more terrestrial toys, I want to invest in things that help others find their way to You.

27

I'M STUMBLING ALONG

TIME has passed, and just when I thought I was doing well . . .

I find myself stumbling along through unfamiliar territory again—overwhelmed and fighting to pull myself together.

It's all these emotions. Sometimes I feel raw inside. Sometimes I'm flooded with loneliness or fear. My nerves are easily frayed, and I can react unreasonably. It's hard to think clearly and make logical decisions.

Is this ever going to end?

I wonder where I stand with other people. Are they tired of my struggle? Do they wish I'd go away and "get it together"? Sometimes I "read into" their words and wonder if they're sending me hidden messages like "Just accept your loss, and get over it."

When I placed my trust in God, I thought I'd never go through this inner unsteadiness and uncertainty again. But I can so quickly flip from trust to turmoil . . . from a steady walk to struggling and feeling lost.

And so I reach out to God once again. I need Him to restore me with a steady faith and a constant hope. Rather than listening to the uncertainties that whisper in my own mind, I place my trust in His sure Word:

> The righteous cry out, and the LORD hears them;
> he delivers them from all their troubles. The LORD
> is close to the brokenhearted and saves those who
> are crushed in spirit. A righteous man may have
> many troubles, but the LORD delivers him from
> them all. (Psalm 34:17-19)

> Though a righteous man falls seven times, he rises
> again. (Proverbs 24:16)

> Since ancient times no one has heard, no ear has
> perceived, no eye has seen any God besides you,
> who acts on behalf of those who wait for him.
> (Isaiah 64:4)

> Be still before the LORD and wait patiently for him; . . .
> do not fret—it leads only to evil. (Psalm 37:7-8)

PRAYER

LORD, I need Your strong hand to hold me up . . . the solid rock of Your truth beneath my feet. When everything within me is shaken, act on my behalf . . . and steady me.

28

HELP ME
MAKE DECISIONS

If it was just the loss, that would be hard enough. But all these decisions are staring me in the face. So many people seem to want answers. Not to mention all the personal adjustments that lie ahead for me.

I make some strides spiritually. And then the mail comes, carrying mundane demands. There are more bills to pay. New financial arrangements to be made. Copies of the death certificate to send. Legal red tape. Then there are things around the house that need to be fixed or replaced.

And when I want to turn to the person I relied on for opinions in decision making . . . of course no one is there. Gone is the emotional support and the counsel I counted on. Every decision makes me feel how alone I am.

I turn to God now and ask His help in making good decisions. I'm ready to accept God's assistance however He sends it—

in the form of an old friend, or a kind and compassionate new acquaintance who recognizes my need. I'm ready to depend directly on God or to recognize and accept His generosity and offer of help through other people.

As I open my eyes, I will live aware that the Lord's assistance often comes from unexpected places. I will look hopefully for His provision. I trust that His wisdom will come to me, enabling me to make sensible choices. And I take His words at face value:

> Trust in the LORD with all your heart and lean not on your own understanding; in all your ways acknowledge him, and he will make your paths straight. (Proverbs 3:5-6)

> If any of you lacks wisdom, he should ask God, who gives generously to all without finding fault, and it will be given to him. (James 1:5)

PRAYER

LORD, I definitely lack wisdom. And I ask You to supply it however You will. I trust You to be my Light for the path, day after day.

29

WAS MY DEAR ONE READY TO MEET GOD?

SOMETHING has troubled me: Is the one I loved really with the Lord? Was the person I miss so much ready to meet God?

These questions haunt me day and night. Uncertainty is a most unwelcome companion. I'm so accustomed to *doing* something to change a situation or to get answers, but there is nothing I can do about this, no place to go for sure answers.

And so I must leave this matter to God. His Word says that each of us is "destined to die once, and after that to face judgment" (Hebrews 9:27). Knowing this, I cast my faith-lot in with the patriarch Abraham, who asked with confidence, "Will not the Judge of all the earth do right?" (Genesis 18:25). I hang on to God's promise that He "is patient with [us], not wanting anyone to perish" (2 Peter 3:9).

Today I stop and consider how intricately God has worked in my life to make me ready for each new step. Confident that

God also prepares each person for death, I can rest, knowing the one I love is in His merciful hands. I will leave the unknowable behind, and walk into the future with my heart fixed on God's truths:

> The secret things belong to the LORD our God,
> but the things revealed belong to us . . . that
> we may follow all the words of this law.
> (Deuteronomy 29:29)

> Let him who walks in the dark, who has no light,
> trust in the name of the LORD and rely on his
> God. . . . The path of the righteous is like the first
> gleam of dawn, shining ever brighter till the full
> light of day. (Isaiah 50:10; Proverbs 4:18)

PRAYER

LORD, I turn over my fears and doubts . . . and place all of life's unknowns into Your hands. I will trust You to guide me from this day forward.

30

WHAT'S LEFT BEHIND IS NOT A "BLESSING"

I never realized how much emotion and trouble can be tied to an inheritance.

Because of sentimental value, a lamp, a watch, a photo album, or a ring suddenly becomes priceless. It's easy to get carried away. Hidden selfishness, greed, jealousy, and old family friction so easily rise to the surface. Why do I have to face *this* kind of crisis when I'm least capable of dealing with it?

I know I need to rely on God's help for this. It will require the wisdom of Solomon, the patience of Job. If my motives include greed, an unwillingness to forgive the past, or thinking only of myself, I need His help so I can change. I also must receive the Lord's wisdom and strength to keep from caving in under the unwarranted pressure others may place on me, openly or subtly.

Mostly, I need God's enabling power to maintain an attitude of forgiveness, so that I won't become overwhelmed by pettiness or greed. Humanly speaking, this can become a real mess. And so I give it to God, resolving to be guided by wisdom from His Word:

> I waited patiently for the LORD; he turned to me and heard my cry. He lifted me out of the slimy pit, out of the mud and mire; he set my feet on a rock and gave me a firm place to stand. . . . Do not withhold your mercy from me, O LORD; may your love and your truth always protect me. For troubles without number surround me. . . . You are my help and my deliverer; O my God, do not delay.
> (Psalm 40:1-2,11-12,17)

PRAYER

LORD, I'm willing to follow Your directions as I resolve estate matters. Each time I must make a decision, please make my course of action plain. Grant me Your peace . . . and Your patience.

BECAUSE I, TOO, MUST FACE ETERNITY

In the days that my loved one has been gone, the finality of death has struck me so many times . . . sometimes with relentless force.

I contemplate these thoughts: When death comes, there is no longer a chance to voice a final apology. No longer an opportunity to make peace with God. No possibility of fulfilling good intentions. No last chance to live a loving life.

I also realize this: At any moment I could make my exit from this life. Like the one I miss so much, my time will come to die. Because I, too, must face eternity, I have to consider: *What will I say to God?*

"I loved *most* of my neighbors." "I kept *some* of Your commandments." "I did my best . . . most of the time."

Can I really stand before God, knowing that I live every day with mixed motives, subtle selfishness, a cutting tongue? Can

I have a clear conscience when I know full well that I often make promises I never intend to keep? That I trust in my material possessions more than I trust in Him? That many of the services I offer Him and others are done grudgingly or half-heartedly?

Today I recall that when Jesus spoke with Nicodemus, a religious man who undoubtedly did more "good deeds" than I ever thought of, He said, "I tell you the truth, no one can see the kingdom of God unless he is born again" (John 3:3). When a crowd of people asked Jesus, "What must we do to do the works God requires?" Jesus answered, "The work of God is this: to believe in the one he has sent" (John 6:28-29).

And so, as I prepare for eternity I must take seriously what God has said. I accept His words as truths to base my life—my eternity—upon:

> God made [Jesus] who had no sin to be sin for us, so that in him we might become the righteousness of God. (2 Corinthians 5:21)

> For it is by grace you have been saved, through faith—and this not from yourselves, it is the gift of God—not by works, so that no one can boast. (Ephesians 2:8-9)

> He saved us, not because of righteous things we had done, but because of his mercy. (Titus 3:5)

PRAYER

LORD, I thank You that salvation depends on Your grace and mercy . . . not on my goodness. I ask for Your forgiveness for the wrongs I've done and for the good I've left undone. Today, and every day, I ask that Your love, wisdom, and strength may be known to others through me. Let others learn to say—because they see You at work in me—He restores my soul!

EPILOGUE:
HOPE FOR ETERNITY

IT might be that in this time of sorrow, you've been forced to reflect on life and death and have come to the conclusion that you're not prepared to meet God. A sincere, heartfelt prayer can change all that. You have God's promises:

> [Jesus speaking] "I tell you the truth, whoever hears my word and believes him who sent me has eternal life and will not be condemned; he has crossed over from death to life." (John 5:24)

> Yet to all who received him [Jesus], to those who believed in his name, he gave the right to become children of God. (John 1:12)

> And this is the testimony: God has given us eternal life, and this life is in his Son. He who has the Son

has life; he who does not have the Son of God does not have life. I write these things to you who believe in the name of the Son of God so that you may know that you have eternal life.
(1 John 5:11-13)

MY PRAYER

GOD, I recognize Your absolute holiness, Your perfection, and Your right to tell me what to do. I admit my failure, my wrongdoing, my rebellion, and my total inability to save myself. At last I recognize that You sent Jesus to die for me and that He shed His blood to take away my sins. Forgive me and cleanse my heart. I detest my disobedience to You and turn from my wayward ways. Relying on the power of Your Holy Spirit living within me, I purpose to obey Your commandments.

LORD, I give my life to you. Invade my being and take full control. I hand over to You my past with its failures and frustrations, my present with its problems and projects—and my hopes and dreams. Perform the miracle of making me into the person You want me to be, one who is ready to spend eternity with You.

LORD, I thank You for taking away my sins, for coming into my heart, and for giving me eternal life. Thank You that now I'm not only ready to die but ready to live. You will be my Companion in grief and in joy, in sickness and in health, in prosperity and in want, for the rest of my life—and beyond.

ABOUT
THE AUTHOR

LORRAINE PETERSON was born in Red Wing, Minnesota. She attended North Park College in Chicago where she received a B.A. in history with a minor in Spanish. She has taken additional courses at the University of Minnesota, the University of Mexico in Mexico City, and the University of Arizona's extension program in Guadalajara, Mexico.

She has taught grades 7–12 in Glenview, Illinois, Minneapolis, Minnesota, and Guadalajara, Mexico. Her first book was published in 1980. She now makes her living as an author and resides in Juárez, Mexico, where she does volunteer writing in Spanish for her church and enjoys the life enrichment that being bilingual and bicultural provides.

THESE RESOURCES WILL HELP YOU TURN NEGATIVES INTO POSITIVES!

Trusting God

It's easy to trust God when everything's going your way. But what about when things go wrong? How do you keep faith in God when you have a tragic car accident, lose a job, or discover you have cancer? This book will teach you how to trust God completely, even in the face of adversity.

Trusting God (Jerry Bridges) $12

The Cry of the Soul

Do you fight off your feelings as if they were enemies? Often our attempts to control our emotions are really a form of rebellion against God or an attempt to flee from Him. This book will encourage you to embrace your negative emotions—anger, jealousy, fear—to reveal truths about God and gain a more intimate relationship with Him.

The Cry of the Soul (Dan B. Allender and Tremper Longman III) $18

Get your copies today at your local bookstore, visit our website at www.navpress.com, or call (800) 366-7788 and ask for offer **#6105** or a FREE catalog of NavPress products.

NAVPRESS
BRINGING TRUTH TO LIFE
www.navpress.com

Prices subject to change.